TO THE MOON

TRISHITA DEY

ISBN 979-888606099-7

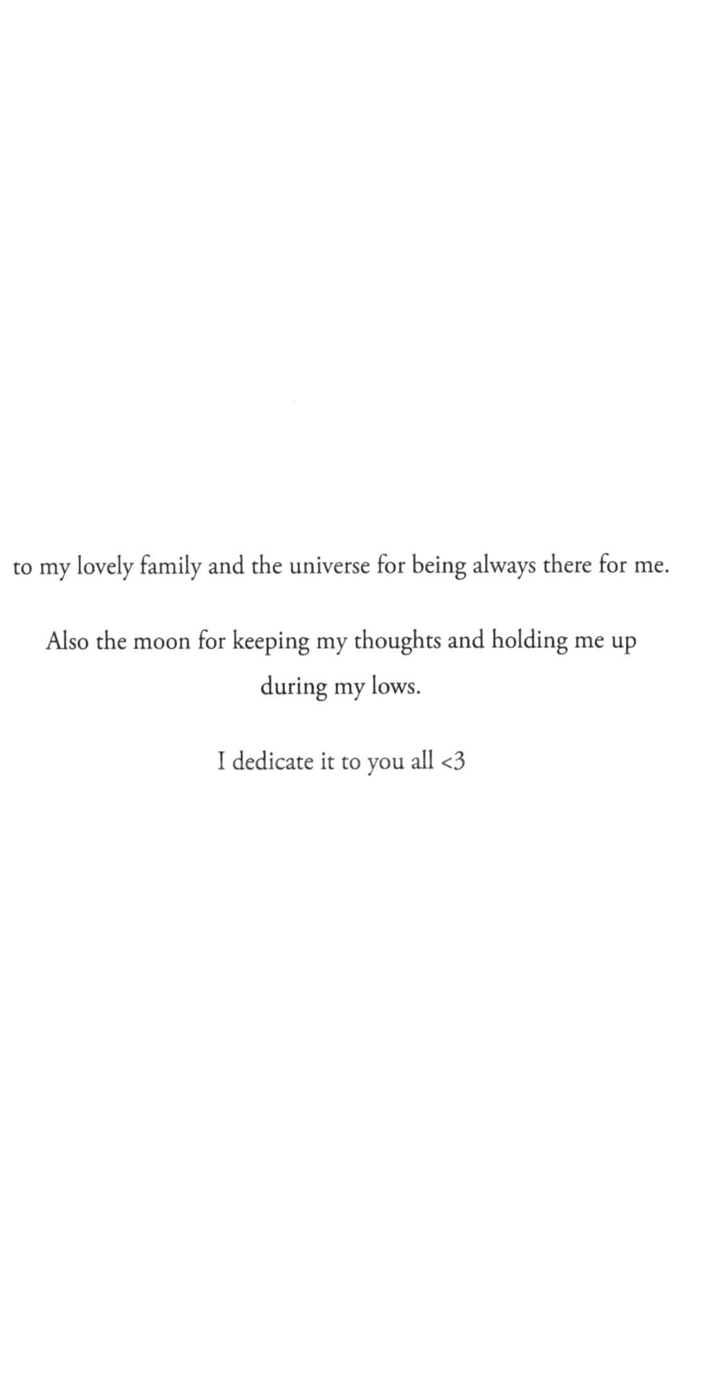

to my lovely family and the universe for being always there for me.

Also the moon for keeping my thoughts and holding me up
during my lows.

I dedicate it to you all <3

Contents

Contents

Preface

Life's a big story and every line of it has some teachings. We experience so much and once in being 18th there's one heartbreak that changes us - changes us for being the better and fills us with experiences. Some cry day and night and feel like it's impossible to forget while others start dating within a week. That's how things happen but you know it's not the end. If someone left you, it's for your betterment. Maybe at that moment you don't feel any good as you only focus on the sad vibration. But trust me, things fall into place and everything becomes clear and you better get to learn from it. Prioritize yourself and see the difference. Never make someone so important that it harms your mental state. You're important and self love is most important. We can't waste our precious time for someone who's temporary. You feel sad - cry cry cry.it's okay to validate your feelings but don't waste the other days. Rather tie up your hair and get done all the tasks you need to do. You're worth all the happiness the universe got to offer, so why be sad?

In this book, I have written poems based on different phases of breakup and finally getting out of it. You all deserve much more than just being the guilty for no reason. I hope you all will relate and if you like my book, do share it with your friends dealing through heart breaks.

Happy Reading everyone!

Chapter1

yes, I was down, hurt, and had endless nights crying.
in a month, couldn't realize how much priority I have given you.
Isn't that why the teacher taught us in mid-school
that first person is always - I
- You matters

Chapter2

Stop coming back to me
like an amusement park
you visit
during vacation.

Chapter3

You tell me that you've loved?
How can I believe that?
after beholding
how you went to date her
just the day we got
over.
- how can you be so quick?

Chapter4

could you please explain my heart, how foolish I am. Trusting in the words of someone, who keeps on faking. How can you be so deceptive is what I feel but ignoring your nuisance again, to make you stay. How can I unseen the seen you, that you have shown. How can I be so forgiven?
But Mumma says forgiving is a superpower.
while I forget everything that you do behind me. Is that what foolishness appears when you're so-called in love?
- *forgive but why silly brain you forget*

Chapter5

With every promise you made,
and the forever words you spoke.
It was all empty
because you meant
nothing.
- I kept on believing you.

Chapter6

Isn't it funny

we seek for forever

in the people

who are just

temporary

- please maturity hit me up

Chapter7

dear 16 y/o me,
I know how drastic you were at the time. How easily you trusted him, how in a month he showed his color to you. It was hard how you dealt with your mental traumas - the deepest secrets and mournful days. You had you by your side, you kept yourself up, you kept looking forward. I am proud of how you managed things. Never feel drenched for that shit, he wasn't worth it, of your love. He felt of you leaving, so he left. He knew how incapable he is.
- keep going dear self, he isn't worth it

Chapter8

You have always tried
but how can you make someone stay
when they're leaving
- the train arrived quite early

Chapter9

I remember all the waves of laughter I had while having
conversations with you
never thought that all
my butterflies would turn into a
forever kind of ache in
my body
- never knew you mastered the art of camouflage

Chapter10

Do you remember me
when you touch her?
Do you feel the
same perfume
when you smell her?
- ***do you remember me?***

Chapter11

With all the hopes in my eyes,
I texted, " I miss you".
" IMY" popped up on the screen
I understood how the love was fading.
It was a revert back and
not a longing.
Quite well you also
mastered the art of
faking
- I wonder what was real

Chapter12

I was in the sea.
Thought it's calm.
Never knew how the
tsunami would
turn me
upside down

Chapter13

You told me that you love me to the moon
but here we go now.
I am writing this book,
with all the scars
you have given
to me.

Chapter14

Drastically it was everything which
didn't even mean anything.
- faking memories

Chapter15

you have been a dreadful nightmare.
The worst of everything I could probably say.
I wish I could redo every memories we had
and hoped that we never met

Chapter16

Mom asked, "Why do you look so weird these days?"
I had no answer. Is that the impact of a heart break?
Being a terrible liar, said," I was just a bit tired".
Mom without wasting a moment after hearing my response replied." Are you in love?"
- Is love always painful?

Chapter17

Do you like to see me cry every time?
Tell me am I that worst?
Wasn't you the one who always said
I would never let your kohl smudge.
- where are you now?

Chapter18

The essence that you gave me is something that I can never forget.
The colors that you gave to my life brought a rainbow.
But the moment, I got to see
it was all a lie,
I felt the rainbow turning
into a thunderstorm

Chapter19

What was the future, you said you saw with me?
Definitely, maybe it was uncertainty and you quite played it well.

Chapter20

So tell me, when you touched me
was that only a part of your game
or did you even mean
a bit anything?
- I am not a doll

Chapter21

Please be normal to me,
it's hard to understand all the complexities you bring up.
It's no more an arguement.
It's suffocating.
It's toxic.

Chapter22

How can you forget everything that has happened?
Every word you spoke and wrote.
Did you remember how you made a song for me
and now you use it for someone else.
I don't understand.
Is that the duality?
Quite well, you forget things.
Like it has never happened.

Chapter23

It all felt cute when you mentioned those
names for me,
now I believe you call her
by the same name?
- don't you have a heart?

Chapter24

See you were the one who always told
together and forever.
Look how bad you are in keeping
your own words.

Chapter25

Thank you for coming into my life. Teaching me all the lessons, surely I won't be able to find them on any educational sites. Thank you for teaching me the kind of people to encounter. Well, I realized enough how stupid I was back then, no doubt I was just 16. Though this was interesting you know, how you lied and I believed, you kept on doing that but always had a guilt mark on me and at last left. As I was the one dating some other. While you didn't even take a week's break to move on to somebody else. Surely, you're so great at all this. It was definitely important for me to have great strength and not look on such jerks.

Now I am flourishing and blooming. Doing far better than what you might be doing. Well, I have no threads anymore, you were quite a headache but you know, I am over you long back. Just a piece of advice, GO GET A LIFE BRO.

Chapter26

I don't need your back
anymore.
When I needed them most,
you went away.
Believe me, I got
to explore myself
and discovering
out my inner peace
and potential
And hell yes!
I can stand alone.
I don't need your back
anymore.

Chapter27

I'm me. Maybe not the same as what I was when 16y/o. Life is not just laid out instructions with perfection. It's the imperfection that makes me so alluring and the several trial and errors are the measures of learning in this race not an epitome of failure.

Chapter28

Astounded in a swift way
how delighting the sun rays.
What can be the best bargains
rather than watching
a gleaming
sun set?
Life escorts you
with a tons of
dictated jagged lessons.
But whatever you get
flap your wings
and dream high

Chapter29

Even you know
it's heartbreaking,
It completely
destructed
you.
You're done with
the scenario
that you're
withstanding.
Just for once
think that after
the dark sky
there comes a
time when
again the sun
comes out.

Chapter30

You're worth more than getting love from an apathetic man.

Chapter31

The day she broke all her cords,
bonds and
delusional mind,
she was free

Chapter32

You're out of the league now

Chapter33

She's grown. she's working
and she is living her life
to the best.
You were the trash that got
settled down at the
right time.
- you left and it was the best thing that happened

Chapter34

Love is always not painful,
but we define love to someone
in words, we personify it.
Clearly a jerk can't define love

Chapter35

She's your biggest regret now.
Well, do settle with the ordinary show-off
case you have.

Chapter36

What's meant to be will happen
and definitely, it will happen
for your highest good.
If it's a breakup,
it's for your own good.
There have been a lot of red flags
that you missed out on.
Never judge the life
for some random clowns.

Chapter37

I never knew how simple things can also be complicated.
You played well, no doubt.

Chapter38

Your void is no more haunting me.
In the process, I found me.
- it's a win

Chapter39

Love should be simple.
Not unclear words and dishonesty.
Mixed signals should always be a no.
You should never play with
your mental health for some
guys who got no life.
- you deserve a healthy relation.

Chapter40

I hope you don't spend all the time feeling sorry.
Darling, it's not your fault.
Stop feeling guilty.
You can't be the victim
of a manipulative guy.
You're powerful and
kind,
Universe will send
you the
love you put
in there.
- don't loose faith

Letter From The Author

Dear readers,

Thank you for coming up to this page - surely you read it. Basically, I tried to create something on a general topic of breakup: how often we fall in love, get hurt, learn, and be the better version of yourselves. You all deserve so much in your life. It's the beginning and you have miles to go! I am very grateful to everyone who read this tiny book. All I wanted is to revert back as I haven't written anything for long. So keep smiling, take care of yourselves and your loved ones.I promise, I will keep getting better with my works and you can always put a review. I literally go through them, they help me to learn.

Sending you all love and lights,

Trishita Dey

9 798886 060997

Printed by Libri Plureos GmbH in Hamburg, Germany